ABDO
Publishing Company

Hiking

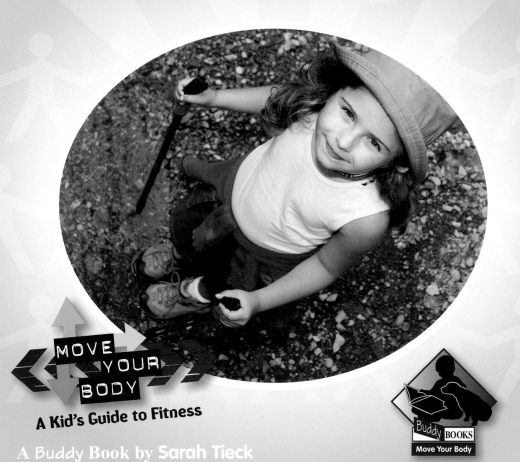

MOVE YOUR BODY

A Kid's Guide to Fitness

A Buddy Book by **Sarah Tieck**

Buddy **BOOKS**
Move Your Body

VISIT US AT
www.abdopublishing.com

Published by ABDO Publishing Company, PO Box 398166, Minneapolis, MN 55439.

Copyright © 2013 by Abdo Consulting Group, Inc. International copyrights reserved in all countries. No part of this book may be reproduced in any form without written permission from the publisher. Buddy Books™ is a trademark and logo of ABDO Publishing Company.

Printed in the United States of America, North Mankato, Minnesota.
102012
012013

 PRINTED ON RECYCLED PAPER

Coordinating Series Editor: Rochelle Baltzer
Contributing Editors: Stephanie Hedlund, Marcia Zappa
Graphic Design: Jenny Christensen
Cover Photograph: *Shutterstock*: Gorilla.
Interior Photographs/Illustrations: *Eighth Street Studio* (p. 26); *Getty Images*: Sri Maiava Rusden (p. 15); *Glow Images*: Superstock (p. 11); *iStockphoto*: ©iStockphoto.com/ Crisma (p. 5), ©iStockphoto.com/eurobanks (p. 23), ©iStockphoto.com/gbh007 (p. 13), ©iStockphoto.com/joel-t (p. 27), ©iStockphoto.com/omgimages (p. 25), ©iStockphoto. com/skynesher (p. 21); *Shutterstock*: Jakub Cejpek (p. 7), Jim David (p. 15), sonya etchison (p. 5), LeventeGyori (p. 26), maga (p. 17), Maridav (p. 30), Tyler Olson (p. 30), PhotoSky 4t com (p. 9), Mark Poprocki (p. 19), Richard Susanto (p. 29), YorkBerlin (p. 13).

Library of Congress Cataloging-in-Publication Data

Tieck, Sarah, 1976-
  Hiking / Sarah Tieck.
      p. cm. -- (Move your body: a kid's guide to fitness)
  ISBN 978-1-61783-562-9 (hardcover)
  1. Hiking--Juvenile literature. I. Title.
  GV199.52.T54 2013
  796.51--dc23
                          2012032934

Table of Contents

Healthy Living

Your body is amazing! A healthy body helps you feel good and live well. In order to be healthy, you must take care of yourself. One way to do this is to move your body.

Regular movement gives you **energy** and makes you stronger. Many kinds of exercise can help you do this. One fun type of exercise is hiking! Let's learn more about hiking.

Some people hike deep in forests. Others hike on city sidewalks.

Hiking 101

Hikers move their bodies over different kinds of land. They walk with their feet and legs. They swing their hands and arms. And, they use their **abdominal** and back **muscles** for balance.

Hikes can be long or short. Some can even last for several weeks! Hikes can also be easy or hard. This depends on where you hike and how fast you move.

Hiking is part of many other activities, such as mountain climbing.

Walking is the most basic form of hiking. You could start by walking in an open area or a park.

As you grow stronger, you can **challenge** yourself. You could hike on steeper trails or go for longer hikes. Someday, you could hike up a mountain!

WORD OF MOUTH

People hike all year long. In the winter, many hikers also cross-country ski.

Hikers must carry packs for long hikes.

Let's Get Physical

People exercise to stay fit. Hiking is a type of **aerobic** exercise. It makes your **lungs** and heart work hard to get your body more **oxygen**. The more you hike, the easier it will be to breathe and move.

Regular hikes can reduce **stress**. They can help you stay at a healthy body weight. This helps prevent health problems later in life.

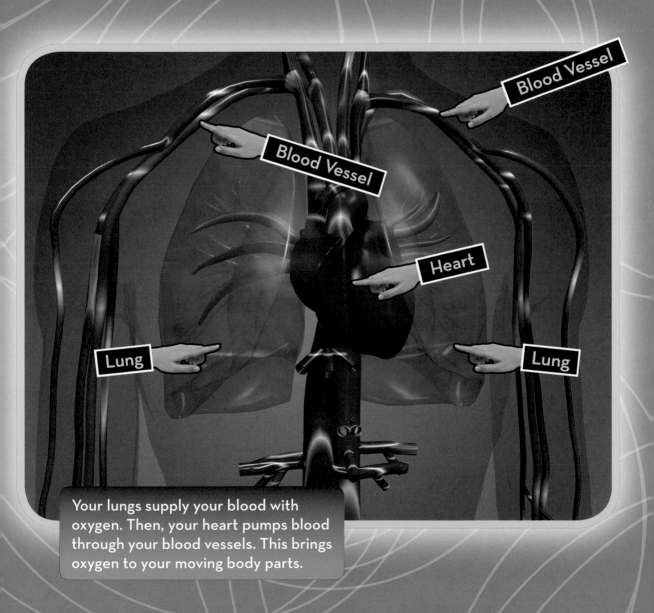

Blood Vessel

Blood Vessel

Heart

Lung

Lung

Your lungs supply your blood with oxygen. Then, your heart pumps blood through your blood vessels. This brings oxygen to your moving body parts.

Hiking also builds **muscle**, especially in your legs. When you walk or climb a hill, you work your leg muscles. Over time, they get stronger and can move more easily.

Gluteus

Quadriceps

Hamstring Muscles

Calf Muscle

Hiking is an exercise that makes your bones stronger!

WORD OF MOUTH

Hiking works different leg muscles. Hiking uphill is extra work for the gluteus and calf muscles.

Gearing Up

To hike, dress in comfortable clothes that are right for the weather. Wear lightweight boots or sneakers. These will help you walk safely on uneven ground.

Many tools can help you while hiking. These include a compass or GPS, a map, and a first-aid kit. Hiking sticks can be helpful for balance. And, they help **protect** your knees and back. They can also be used to push plants aside.

A raincoat helps keep you dry in rain.

Be sure to pack water and food for your hike!

A compass shows you what direction you are facing. A GPS shows your exact location. Orienteering is a hiking sport that uses a map and a compass. Geocaching is similar, but uses a GPS.

WORD OF MOUTH

Play It Safe

Hiking can be unsafe. Trails may be steep. Sometimes tree roots or branches lay across them. This could cause you to trip and fall. So, you must pay attention to your surroundings.

Bugs and sun are part of nature. Wear bug spray and sunscreen when you hike. This **protects** you from bug bites and sunburn.

Many hiking trails have uneven ground. This can make walking difficult.

Every year, many people are hurt while hiking. They may fall or get hurt in other ways. Some even have to stay in the hospital for a couple days.

So, it is important to be careful when you hike. Always hike with a group, buddies, or your family. And, tell an adult where you are going and when you will return.

WORD OF MOUTH

A cell phone can be an important safety tool. Be sure to bring one on a hike. But, silence your ringer so you don't disturb others in the area.

Hiking on marked trails helps you stay safe.

Ready? Set? Go!

Warm up for a hike by doing some slow movements like bending. This prepares your **muscles** to work hard. Cool down after hiking by slowing your pace. This helps keep your muscles from getting sore.

Stretching is also an important part of exercise. Over time, it can make you more **flexible**. This makes it easier for your body to move.

Hikers often stretch their legs after warming up and after hiking.

Look and Learn

There are many cool things to see in nature. Watch for plants, animals, and land formations. Some plants are harmful. So if you are unfamiliar with a plant, don't touch it.

Good manners are important when you hike. Be sure to talk softly when others are around. Don't play loud music. Walk on marked trails and obey signs. And when you leave, bring your garbage with you to throw away.

Don't take rocks or flowers from their original spot. Instead, bring a camera on your hike. Take pictures of the cool things you see!

WORD OF MOUTH

Bring paper and a pencil on a hike to draw what you see.

It is also important to pay attention to the weather. Don't hike during a storm or when there's lightning. If storm clouds form while you hike, head home quickly.

If a storm happens while you hike, find a fully enclosed building or vehicle. If you can't, take shelter under low trees or behind low boulders. Stay away from open fields, tall hills or ridges, water, and metal.

If you are staying overnight, be sure to make a plan. Bring enough food and other supplies to stay safe.

Brain Food

How do you know if you are hiking hard enough to get a workout?

Some people just pay attention to how their bodies feel. Others measure their heart rate. This is the number of times your heart beats per minute.  A tool called a heart rate monitor measures this. You can also find this on your own. Touch the inside of your wrist. Then, count the pulses you feel in one minute.

I'm afraid I'll get hurt or lost while hiking. What can I do?

Never hike alone. Make a plan before you go on a hike. Carry supplies, such as water and a first-aid kit, in case you need them. You should also pack a whistle. Blow it if you are in trouble so people can hear it and find you.

I want to get ready for a long hike. What can I do to prepare?

Groups such as Boy Scouts and Girl Scouts teach hiking skills. Troop members go on nature walks. You could also hike with your family in areas close to home. Make your hike a bit longer each time to grow stronger.

Choose to Move

Remember that hiking makes your body stronger. Hike as often as you can. Fitness is an important part of a healthy life. Each positive choice you make will help you stay healthy.

Hiking is good for your body. Seeing forests, waterfalls, and other natural places is fun! Some people call it an adventure.

KEEP SAFE

✔ Learn about plants such as poison ivy, poison oak, and poison sumac. They can make you itchy. So, look but don't touch or eat!

✔ When you hike, wear sunscreen to **protect** your skin.

DRINK UP

✔ Carry a water bottle when you hike. It is not safe to drink water you find in nature.

✔ Water plays an important part in helping your body build **muscle**. So, be sure to drink some before, during, and after a hike.

LEARN MORE

✔ Set a **goal** to improve your hiking. Distance or time are ways to measure progress.

✔ Try geocaching! To do this, you use a GPS to find different locations.

Important Words

abdominal relating to the part of the body between the chest and the hips.

aerobic (ehr-OH-bihk) relating to exercise that increases oxygen in the body and makes the heart better able to use oxygen.

challenge (CHA-luhnj) to test one's strengths or abilities.

energy (EH-nuhr-jee) the power or ability to do things.

flexible able to bend or move easily.

goal something that a person works to reach or complete.

lungs body parts that help the body breathe.

muscle (MUH-suhl) body tissue, or layers of cells, that helps move the body.

oxygen (AHK-sih-juhn) a colorless gas that humans and animals need to breathe.

protect (pruh-TEHKT) to guard against harm or danger.

stress a feeling of worry that may lead to some illnesses.

Web Sites

To learn more about hiking, visit ABDO Publishing Company online. Web sites about hiking are featured on our Book Links page. These links are routinely monitored and updated to provide the most current information available.

www.abdopublishing.com

Index